# Becoming an AI-First Organization

Paramendra Kumar Bhagat

www.paramendra.com

# Table Of Contents

# Book Outline

## Becoming an AI-First Organization

### Chapter 1: The AI Revolution Has Arrived

- The rise of AI as the next foundational technology

- Comparing AI to the internet, electricity, and fire

- Why now is the inflection point for AI adoption

- Case studies of early adopters and laggards

### Chapter 2: Defining "AI-First"

- What "AI-first" truly means

- Beyond buzzwords: AI as an operating philosophy

- AI-first vs. AI-enabled vs. AI-curious organizations

- Mindset shifts required at leadership and team levels

### Chapter 3: Culture Eats Technology for Breakfast

- Rethinking corporate culture in the age of AI

- How to build a culture of curiosity, experimentation, and agility

- Encouraging collaboration between humans and machines

- Avoiding fear-based resistance

## Chapter 4: The Productivity Multiplier

- Automating repetitive tasks with AI agents

- From time savings to intelligence amplification

- Examples: AI in scheduling, reporting, research, and analysis

- Empowering each team member with AI "co-pilots"

## Chapter 5: Communication and Innovation in the AI Era

- AI-enhanced collaboration and communication tools

- Using AI to accelerate brainstorming, ideation, and decision-making

- Real-world examples of innovation driven by AI insights

- Cross-functional collaboration in AI-first teams

## Chapter 6: Unlocking New Growth Frontiers

- AI as a growth enabler: smarter marketing, personalized outreach, predictive sales

- Scaling operations with AI without adding headcount

- Platform thinking and AI-powered business models

- Case studies: From startups to enterprises

## Chapter 7: The Democratization of AI

- How small and medium businesses can lead the AI charge

- Low-cost and no-code tools making AI accessible

- Case studies: SMBs transforming with chatbots, automation, and analytics

- Local, regional, and global opportunities

## Chapter 8: Laying the Groundwork: Phase One

- Conducting an AI-readiness audit

- Identifying low-hanging fruit for initial AI adoption

- Creating pilot projects and early wins

- Setting realistic expectations

## Chapter 9: Scaling AI Across the Organization

- Moving from pilots to platforms

- AI adoption across marketing, HR, finance, operations, and support

- Creating internal AI champions and innovation labs

- Governance and change management best practices

## Chapter 10: Reimagining Business Processes from Scratch

- Designing workflows around AI, not retrofitting

- Intelligent automation vs. traditional automation

- Human-in-the-loop systems and ethical safeguards

- Reskilling your workforce for the future

## Chapter 11: AI Ethics, Trust, and Accountability

- Responsible AI use and data governance

- Transparency, bias mitigation, and model explainability

- Creating ethical AI policies and training modules

- Regulatory trends and compliance

## Chapter 12: The AI-First Future

- The competitive advantage of becoming AI-first

- Visionary leadership and long-term thinking

- Building antifragile organizations

- Your 1-year, 3-year, and 10-year roadmap

# Chapter 1: The AI Revolution Has Arrived

## Introduction: Welcome to the Age of Intelligence

Every few decades, humanity encounters a technological leap so transformative that it rewrites the rules of business, culture, and society itself. The combustion engine. Electricity. The internet. Each of these changed the fabric of civilization. Today, we are witnessing the dawn of another such moment: the Age of Artificial Intelligence.

AI is no longer science fiction. It is science fact, and it is reshaping everything from how we work and communicate to how we build products, deliver services, and manage organizations. For businesses, this is not just a trend. It is the *tectonic shift* of the 21st century.

## 1.1 From Novelty to Necessity

In the early 2000s, AI was the stuff of labs and PhDs. In the 2010s, it became a strategic edge for tech giants. Today, in the 2020s, AI is becoming table stakes for every serious organization — regardless of size, sector, or geography.

What changed?

- **Explosion of Data**: Businesses now collect vast amounts of structured and unstructured data, ripe for intelligent analysis.

- **Computational Power**: Cloud infrastructure and GPUs made it economically feasible to train large AI models.

- **Breakthroughs in Algorithms**: From neural nets to transformers, AI systems now rival or exceed human performance in specific tasks.

- **Democratization of Tools**: With tools like ChatGPT, Midjourney, and low-code AI platforms, anyone can now leverage AI — not just data scientists.

The shift is real. The AI revolution has arrived.

## 1.2 AI as a Foundational Technology

AI is not a tool. It is not an app. It is not a feature. **It is a foundational layer**, akin to:

- **Electricity**: Powering countless invisible systems behind the scenes.

- **The Internet**: Reshaping communication, commerce, and culture.

- **The Wheel**: A simple invention with exponential consequences.

To be AI-first means to build *on top of* this layer — not to add it as an afterthought.

## 1.3 Why This Matters Now

Why the urgency? Why are organizations scrambling to become AI-ready?

Because we've reached **the tipping point**.

- **Cost of Inaction is Rising**: Falling behind in AI now means becoming obsolete later. AI-first competitors are already pulling ahead.

- **Speed of Innovation is Accelerating**: What took five years to develop in 2018 can be built in five months today.

- **Consumer Expectations Have Changed**: Instant answers. Personalized experiences. Predictive interactions. AI is no longer impressive; it's expected.

## 1.4 Industries Already Transformed

Let's look at sectors already feeling the full impact of AI:

**Healthcare**

- AI-assisted diagnostics (radiology, pathology)

- Drug discovery acceleration (e.g., DeepMind's AlphaFold)

- Virtual health assistants and symptom checkers

**Finance**

- Fraud detection using machine learning

- AI-driven portfolio management (robo-advisors)

- Risk modeling and insurance underwriting

**Retail**

- Personalized product recommendations

- Dynamic pricing engines

- Demand forecasting and inventory automation

**Manufacturing**

- Predictive maintenance of machinery

- AI-powered supply chain optimization

- Robotics with embedded vision and feedback systems

**Media & Entertainment**

- AI-generated content, scripts, and video (e.g., Sora)

- Audience analytics and hyper-targeted advertising

- Deepfake detection and IP protection

## 1.5 The Winners Are Building AI-Native Operations

Take a look at the fastest-growing companies of the last decade — Amazon, Google, Tesla, TikTok, OpenAI. What do they all have in common?

They treat AI as **a core competency**, not a side project.

They do not merely *use* AI. They build **AI-native operations**, where:

- Every decision is informed by machine intelligence.

- Every customer touchpoint is enhanced by personalization.

- Every workflow is automated, optimized, and scaled.

They are **AI-first by design**, not by accident.

## 1.6 AI Democratized: Why Every Business Can Now Compete

The good news? You don't need billions in R&D to ride this wave.

Thanks to open-source models, cloud APIs, and SaaS platforms, *every* organization can begin adopting AI now. This includes:

- A 5-person digital agency automating client proposals.

- A mid-sized law firm using GPT to summarize case law.

- A global logistics firm using AI to optimize last-mile delivery.

The AI revolution is **inclusive** — but only for those who act.

## 1.7 Signs You're Behind

Here are red flags your organization is lagging behind the AI curve:

- Still relying on manual data entry and spreadsheets.

- Customer queries take hours or days to respond to.

- No experimentation with AI chatbots, agents, or copilots.

- Decisions are made on intuition, not data.

- AI is viewed as a "tech department thing."

## 1.8 What Early Adoption Looks Like

So what does good early adoption look like?

- **AI Chatbots** on the company website answering FAQs 24/7.

- **AI Assistants** helping teams generate content, conduct research, and schedule meetings.

- **AI Automation** of backend workflows (e.g., invoice processing, HR onboarding).

- **AI-Powered Analytics** uncovering insights your BI dashboard missed.

These early wins create momentum — and trust — across the company.

## 1.9 The Risk of "Wait and See"

Many leaders are still in *wait-and-see* mode. But here's the truth:

- AI capabilities are improving exponentially, not linearly.

- The longer you wait, the steeper the learning curve.

- Early adopters will shape industry standards and capture market share.

Inaction is no longer neutral. It's strategic regression.

## 1.10 The Paradigm Shift is Cultural, Not Just Technical

Becoming an AI-first organization isn't just about plugging in a model. It's about **rethinking how your company works**:

- How you make decisions.

- How you measure performance.

- How you train employees.

- How you serve customers.

AI-first is as much a cultural transformation as it is a technological one.

## 1.11 Thought Leaders Speak

"AI is the biggest opportunity — and the biggest disruption — since the invention of electricity."
— *Andrew Ng, co-founder of Google Brain*

"The companies that fail to adopt AI will disappear — like Blockbuster in the age of Netflix."
— *Kai-Fu Lee, former president of Google China*

"AI is not going to replace humans. But humans using AI will replace those who don't."
— *Garry Kasparov, former chess world champion*

## 1.12 Call to Action: Begin Now, or Fall Behind

If you're reading this book, chances are you know change is coming. Maybe it's already here. Maybe it's overwhelming. That's okay.

The key is to begin.

- Start with one AI tool.

- Launch one pilot project.

- Get one team onboard.

The AI revolution isn't a single moment. It's a movement — and **it's happening in real-time**. Those who move now will build the future. Those who don't will be disrupted by it.

---

## Conclusion: This Is Your AI Moment

Chapter 1 lays the groundwork for everything that follows. The rest of this book will walk you step-by-step through becoming an AI-first organization — in culture, in operations, in leadership, and in strategy.

The revolution is here.

Are you ready to lead it?

# Chapter 2: Defining "AI-First"

## Introduction: More Than a Buzzword

"AI-First" is one of the most talked-about — and misunderstood — phrases in modern business. Too often, it is tossed around in strategy memos or marketing decks without clarity or conviction. To truly become AI-first, an organization must undergo a **fundamental transformation**: one that reorients its thinking, its workflows, and its purpose around the intelligent use of data and algorithms.

Being AI-first is not simply about *using* AI. It's about *thinking* AI. It's about *building* for AI. It's about *leading* with AI.

This chapter defines what that means.

---

## 2.1 Origins of the Term "AI-First"

The term "AI-First" was popularized by **Sundar Pichai**, CEO of Google, in 2016. At the time, Google was transitioning from being a mobile-first company to an AI-first one. This meant a complete redesign of services like Search, Photos, Translate, and Gmail — all driven by intelligent systems.

Since then, dozens of companies — from startups to Fortune 500s — have begun adopting the AI-first language. But how many have adopted the **AI-first mindset**?

Let's break it down.

---

## 2.2 AI-First vs. AI-Aware vs. AI-Enabled

It's important to distinguish between three often-confused categories of organizations:

**AI-Aware Organizations**

- Curious about AI

- Have held a few workshops or keynotes

- May use AI tangentially (e.g., a chatbot on the site)

- No core AI strategy

**AI-Enabled Organizations**

- Use AI in certain functions (e.g., marketing automation, fraud detection)

- May buy AI solutions from vendors

- Benefit from AI, but haven't restructured for it

**AI-First Organizations**

- Treat AI as a strategic imperative, not a feature

- Design products, workflows, and teams around AI capabilities

- Use proprietary data and in-house models to create competitive moats

- Have AI governance, ethics, and innovation baked into the DNA

---

## 2.3 The AI-First Mindset

To become AI-first, companies must develop a new mental model across five dimensions:

1. **Strategic Thinking**
   View AI as essential infrastructure, not a luxury add-on.

2. **Data-Driven Decision-Making**
   Replace gut instinct with evidence-based automation.

3. **AI as Co-Worker**
   Redesign roles and teams around human-AI collaboration.

4. **Speed of Execution**
   Use AI to iterate faster, deploy smarter, and scale sustainably.

5. **Innovation DNA**
   Prioritize experimentation, model testing, and feedback loops.

---

## 2.4 Organizational Redesign Around AI

AI-first companies often go through structural shifts:

### From Hierarchies to Hybrid Teams

- Traditional org charts give way to agile pods

- Each pod includes domain experts, data engineers, and AI strategists

### From SOPs to Continuous Learning

- Static processes are replaced by self-improving workflows

- AI learns from data; humans learn from AI

### From Top-Down Decisions to Intelligence-Augmented Decisions

- Leaders rely on AI dashboards and predictive analytics

- AI recommends, humans decide

---

## 2.5 Reimagining the Customer Experience

AI-first isn't just internal. It transforms how companies relate to their customers:

- Hyper-personalization of services

- Real-time feedback and product adaptation

- 24/7 conversational interfaces powered by LLMs

- Predictive customer service and sentiment detection

Amazon's "customers who bought this also bought" evolved into AI-first product ecosystems where every interaction feeds back into smarter recommendations and experiences.

---

## 2.6 Rewriting the Tech Stack

Being AI-first requires rethinking the foundational technology layers:

- **Data Infrastructure:** Data lakes, pipelines, and warehouses must be clean, connected, and queryable in real time.

- **Model Architecture:** Use of pre-trained models (like GPT) and fine-tuning for domain-specific tasks.

- **Tooling:** Adoption of MLOps, AutoML, and low-code/no-code platforms for rapid development.

- **APIs and Integrations:** Plug-and-play AI services for translation, speech-to-text, vision, and recommendations.

---

## 2.7 Use Case-Driven AI Strategy

AI-first companies don't adopt tech for the sake of it. They identify *high-impact use cases*, such as:

- Reducing customer churn using predictive analytics

- Improving conversion rates via AI-led A/B testing

- Automating contract review in legal firms

- Detecting anomalies in real-time logistics data

Each use case serves as a beachhead — building momentum for broader transformation.

---

## 2.8 Becoming AI-Native

Eventually, AI-first companies aim to be **AI-native** — organizations whose products could not exist without AI. Examples include:

- TikTok (AI-curated content)

- OpenAI (AI as the product itself)

- Tesla (real-time AI driving systems)

- Grammarly (language AI with feedback loops)

These are not companies using AI. They are companies *enabled by the existence* of AI.

---

## 2.9 How Leaders Think in AI-First Companies

Leadership in AI-first organizations exhibits:

- **Vision:** Clear, long-term commitment to integrating AI into mission-critical operations.

- **Literacy:** Deep understanding of how AI works and where it fits.

- **Risk Tolerance:** Willingness to run pilots, accept failure, and iterate fast.

- **Governance:** Proactive handling of ethics, bias, and transparency.

AI-first leadership is not optional — it's existential.

---

## 2.10 Misconceptions About Being AI-First

Some common myths debunked:

- **"We use AI, so we're AI-first."** → Not unless AI drives strategy.

- **"We have a data science team."** → That's great, but are they embedded in decision loops?

- **"We use ChatGPT internally."** → Nice! But is it integrated into your workflows?

AI-first isn't about isolated innovation. It's about **systemic transformation**.

---

## 2.11 Cultural Shifts Required

You can't bolt AI onto a legacy culture. To be AI-first:

- Replace fear of AI with fluency in AI

- Encourage transparency, not silos

- Reward experimentation over perfection

- Train every employee, not just engineers

Culture change is the real unlock.

---

## 2.12 The Ethical Imperative

An AI-first organization must also be **ethics-first**:

- Bias in models must be measured and mitigated

- Transparent documentation of algorithms (model cards)

- Respect for privacy and data sovereignty

- Governance boards and review cycles for high-stakes use cases

Being AI-first without being responsible is a recipe for backlash.

---

## 2.13 AI-First in Practice: Examples

### Spotify
Uses AI to recommend music, detect trends, and generate personalized playlists — all in real time.

**UPS**

Uses AI to optimize delivery routes, saving millions in fuel costs while cutting emissions.

**Klarna**

AI handles 90% of customer queries automatically — reducing response time and improving satisfaction.

These are not one-time features. These are strategic redesigns.

---

## 2.14 Questions Every Organization Must Ask

- Where in our organization can AI immediately create value?

- What workflows need to be reimagined from an AI-first perspective?

- How do we ensure human-in-the-loop design and oversight?

- What kind of leadership and talent do we need for this journey?

- Are we treating data as an asset or a byproduct?

---

## 2.15 Your AI-First Scorecard

Evaluate your readiness:

| Category | AI-Aware | AI-Enabled | AI-First |
| --- | --- | --- | --- |
| Strategy | Mentioned in slide decks | Pilots in progress | Core to mission |
| Teams | Centralized experts | Department-level use | Cross-functional integration |
| Tools | Vendor demos | One or two solutions | Internal platforms |
| Culture | Curiosity | Experimentation | Fluency and buy-in |
| Governance | N/A | Ad-hoc | Embedded and ethical |

Where are you today? Where do you want to be in 12 months?

## Conclusion: Begin with Definition, End with Transformation

Defining "AI-First" is the most important step before becoming it. It's not enough to have ambition. You need **shared language, shared vision, and shared commitment**.

This chapter is your mirror. It helps you see where you are — and where you need to go.

The next chapters will walk you through **how to build**, **scale**, and **sustain** an AI-first organization — across technology, culture, workflows, and governance.

Let's build the future — one intelligent step at a time.

# Chapter 3: Culture Eats Technology for Breakfast

*"Culture eats strategy for breakfast." – Peter Drucker*

In the age of artificial intelligence, this quote needs a small but vital update:
**Culture eats technology for breakfast — and lunch and dinner, too.**

You can have the best AI models, hire the smartest engineers, and partner with top vendors — but if your culture is outdated, resistant, or fearful, your AI initiative will fail. Culture is the invisible architecture that determines how people think, act, and adapt.

This chapter explores why culture is the make-or-break factor for becoming AI-first — and how you can build one that thrives in an intelligent age.

---

## 3.1 The Myth of "Just Add AI"

Many organizations treat AI like a plugin — just drop it in, and the magic will happen. But without the right culture:

- Employees resist or underutilize AI tools

- Managers fear losing control or status

- Innovation is stifled by legacy thinking

- Data remains siloed and under-leveraged

You don't just *install* AI. You *become* AI-first — and that requires a fundamental cultural shift.

## 3.2 What Is Culture in the Context of AI?

Culture is the **collective mindset** and **behavioral patterns** of an organization. In the AI context, it includes:

- **Attitudes toward experimentation**

- **Comfort with automation and change**

- **Trust in data over hierarchy**

- **Openness to collaboration with machines**

- **A learning orientation at all levels**

Think of culture as the soil in which AI seeds are planted. If the soil is toxic, nothing will grow.

## 3.3 Core Cultural Traits of AI-First Organizations

### 1. Curiosity Over Complacency

- Encouraging questions like: "What can we automate?", "What can AI do better?"

- Embracing failure as part of innovation

- Celebrating experimentation

### 2. Data-Driven by Default

- Replacing opinion-based decisions with evidence-based ones

- Making data accessible to everyone — not just analysts

- Teaching teams how to interpret and act on data

### 3. Comfort with Change

- Building muscle memory for continuous adaptation

- Encouraging agility in structure, roles, and workflows

**4. Collaboration Across Functions**

- AI adoption is not just IT's job

- Cross-disciplinary teams combining domain, data, and design expertise

**5. Ethics, Trust, and Transparency**

- Cultural norms that question, not blindly accept AI output

- Ethical use of AI reinforced by leadership and policy

- Clear communication about where and how AI is used

---

## 3.4 Barriers to Cultural Transformation

Organizations may face the following blockers:

- **Fear of Job Loss:** Employees see AI as a threat, not a tool.

- **Techno-Elitism:** Only "experts" are trusted to touch AI.

- **Legacy Mindsets:** "This is how we've always done it."

- **Lack of Leadership Buy-In:** Culture change starts at the top.

- **Mistrust in AI:** Especially when models are black-box or poorly explained.

Each of these must be acknowledged and addressed with empathy, clarity, and action.

---

## 3.5 The Role of Leadership in Culture Change

AI-first transformation begins and ends with leadership. Effective AI leaders:

- **Model curiosity and vulnerability:** Ask questions, admit what they don't know.

- **Invest in people:** Training, coaching, and mentoring on AI fluency.

- **Break down silos:** Cross-pollinate ideas between departments.

- **Celebrate small wins:** Recognize successful AI use cases, no matter how small.

- **Set ethical tone:** Demand transparency, fairness, and accountability in AI systems.

Leadership is not just about strategy. It's about storytelling, championing, and driving belief.

---

## 3.6 Middle Management: The Critical Leverage Point

Middle managers can make or break cultural change. They often face pressure from above and skepticism from below. Empower them by:

- Equipping them with AI tools for team productivity

- Training them to facilitate change, not enforce it

- Including them in AI governance and roadmap design

- Giving them metrics to track AI integration success

AI-first culture flows through the middle, not just from the top.

---

## 3.7 Empowering the Frontlines

Frontline employees often feel the most exposed to automation. Involve them as *co-creators*, not *casualties*, of change:

- Involve them in AI testing and feedback loops

- Design AI interfaces they can actually use

- Use AI to augment, not replace, their judgment

- Show how AI saves time, reduces stress, and improves outcomes

Example: In a hospital, nurses used to fill out patient notes manually. With voice-enabled AI, they spend more time with patients and less with paperwork.

---

## 3.8 Learning and Upskilling: From Fear to Fluency

A winning culture sees AI not as a threat to jobs — but as a *catalyst for growth*.

**Strategies to Upskill at Scale:**

- Launch AI Literacy Programs: From executives to interns.

- Create AI Champions: Evangelists embedded in every team.

- Offer Learning Pathways: Curated tracks by function and role.

- Host AI Hackathons: Practical, fun, and cross-functional.

- Incentivize Learning: Tie upskilling to recognition and advancement.

Organizations that learn faster, adapt faster.

---

## 3.9 Building Psychological Safety

Innovation requires risk. Risk requires safety.

A culture of psychological safety means:

- Employees can raise concerns about AI ethics

- Teams can test and fail without punishment

- Leaders are open to feedback, especially from below

- AI outputs can be challenged — by humans

This builds trust, and trust is the currency of AI adoption.

---

## 3.10 Measuring Cultural Progress

You can't manage what you can't measure. Track your culture using:

- AI adoption metrics (usage across tools and departments)

- Employee AI sentiment surveys (fear, trust, fluency)

- Cross-functional collaboration rates

- Internal innovation submissions

- Learning and upskilling engagement

These are leading indicators of whether your culture is AI-ready.

---

## 3.11 Case Studies in Culture-Led AI Transformation

### A. Intuit

- Focus on "design for delight" culture

- Every product manager trained in AI experimentation

- AI tools used for taxes, financial planning, and customer success

### B. DBS Bank (Singapore)

- Transformed from a traditional bank to a digital-first, AI-driven culture

- "Culture by design" initiative to embed innovation into daily rituals

- Encouraged employees to identify automation opportunities

### C. Airbnb

- Created internal tools like "Knowledge Repo" to democratize data science

- Hosted internal AI summits and sharing sessions

- Treated AI experimentation like product innovation

## 3.12 Culture as a Living System

Your AI-first culture is never "done." It evolves through:

- Feedback loops from employees and customers

- New technologies and AI capabilities

- Regulatory changes and ethical norms

- Economic, political, and environmental shifts

Think of culture not as a mission statement — but as a **living, adaptive ecosystem**.

## 3.13 The Culture Playbook for AI-First Organizations

| Principle | Practice | Example |
|---|---|---|
| Curiosity | Ask "what if?" daily | Daily AI tip in Slack |
| Accessibility | Simplify AI tools | Low-code dashboards |
| Inclusion | Invite all roles | Warehouse workers in AI pilots |
| Recognition | Celebrate adoption | Monthly "AI Impact" awards |
| Reflection | Pause to learn | Postmortems on failed pilots |

Culture isn't what's written on your walls. It's what your people do when no one's watching.

## 3.14 When Culture Resists: Course Correction Tactics

- Use internal storytelling — success stories of peers who benefited from AI

- Start with small wins in "safe" departments (HR, marketing)

- Bring skeptics into the process — give them real influence

- Don't mandate AI adoption — create pull, not push

Resistance is natural. Inclusion is transformational.

---

## Conclusion: Culture is the Platform

In AI transformation, tech is the hardware. Culture is the operating system. If the OS is outdated, the hardware will crash. But if the OS is resilient, adaptive, and secure, innovation can scale infinitely.

So before you hire your next ML engineer or sign another vendor contract, pause and ask:

- Do your people feel safe with AI?

- Do they feel empowered by it?

- Do they feel included in shaping the future?

Because *that* is the foundation of every AI-first organization.

# Chapter 4: The Productivity Multiplier

## Introduction: Redefining Productivity for the AI Age

For centuries, productivity has been defined by output per unit of input: more goods produced per worker, more code written per hour, more customers served per rep.

But in the AI age, **productivity is no longer about volume**. It's about velocity, precision, personalization, and intelligence. The productivity multiplier offered by AI is unlike anything seen before. It's not a 10% gain — it's often 10x.

AI-first organizations understand that the goal is not just automation — it's **augmentation**. It's not to replace people, but to empower them. This chapter will show how.

---

## 4.1 The Historical Arc of Productivity

- **First Industrial Revolution**: Machines replaced manual labor.

- **Second Industrial Revolution**: Electrification and assembly lines scaled output.

- **Third Industrial Revolution**: Computers and the internet digitized workflows.

- **Fourth Industrial Revolution (Now)**: AI augments thinking, decisions, and creativity.

AI moves productivity from *effort-based* to *intelligence-based*.

---

## 4.2 What Is the AI Productivity Multiplier?

The productivity multiplier refers to **exponential improvements in output, speed, and quality** when AI is integrated across the organization. These include:

- Doing more in less time (velocity)

- Doing it better (quality and accuracy)

- Doing the right things (strategic alignment)

- Doing it with fewer resources (efficiency)

- Doing it with personalization at scale (impact)

It's like giving every employee their own **digital assistant, analyst, researcher, and strategist — all in one**.

---

## 4.3 Three Dimensions of AI-Driven Productivity

### 1. Task Automation

- Repetitive tasks (data entry, scheduling, form processing)

- Example: AI-powered invoice scanning reduces finance team workload by 80%

### 2. Task Augmentation

- AI assists in human work (writing, decision support, diagnostics)

- Example: Legal AI reviews contracts faster and flags anomalies, but lawyers retain judgment

### 3. Task Acceleration

- AI enables teams to work at a pace never possible before

- Example: Product marketing campaigns that took weeks now take hours

---

## 4.4 AI Across Business Functions: Use Cases that Multiply Productivity

### A. Marketing

- AI generates blog posts, email copy, ad headlines

- Personalization engines tailor messaging for each customer

- Predictive analytics identifies high-converting segments

**Example**: A 4-person content team at an eCommerce brand doubled output using AI writing assistants.

### B. Sales

- Lead scoring models prioritize outreach

- Sales bots handle early-stage qualification

- AI-assisted CRM updates reduce admin time

**Example**: One AI-first SaaS firm saw a 40% increase in conversions with AI-prompted talk tracks.

### C. Human Resources

- Resume parsing and matching for open roles

- Sentiment analysis for employee feedback

- AI-driven learning recommendations

**Example**: An AI-powered internal job board improved internal mobility and reduced attrition by 25%.

### D. Customer Support

- Chatbots answer FAQs 24/7

- AI detects emotion and urgency in support tickets

- Smart routing improves first-contact resolution

**Example**: A bank reduced Tier 1 support costs by 60% with an LLM-powered chatbot.

## E. Operations & Logistics

- AI forecasts demand and adjusts procurement

- Predictive maintenance for machinery

- Route optimization for delivery fleets

**Example**: A global supply chain saved $5M/year by avoiding delays through AI-driven rerouting.

## F. Finance & Accounting

- Auto-categorization of expenses

- Real-time risk analysis and fraud detection

- AI-generated financial summaries and forecasts

**Example**: An AI-first CFO spends 80% less time on quarterly reporting and 10x more on strategy.

---

# 4.5 The Compound Effect of Layering AI Tools

Individually, each tool might save a few hours a week. Collectively, they unlock exponential capacity:

- 1 employee x 10 tools = a super-employee

- 1 team x 10 AI agents = a startup that punches above its weight

- 1 org x AI-first thinking = a category-defining company

Compound AI effects are like compound interest: subtle at first, then unstoppable.

---

# 4.6 AI Copilots: The New Normal

AI copilots work *alongside* humans in real time:

- Coders use GitHub Copilot for faster development

- Writers use GPT-based tools to overcome writer's block

- Analysts use natural language BI to query data

- Designers use AI tools to generate visuals or suggest layouts

AI copilots don't replace professionals — they elevate them.

---

## 4.7 Micro-Productivity Gains, Macro-Organizational Impact

Small productivity wins at the individual level aggregate to massive impact:

- A 5% boost per employee x 1,000 employees = 50 full-time equivalents unlocked

- A 10-minute daily time-saving x 300 days = 50 extra hours/year/person

- Multiply that across teams, and you gain entire *months* of extra capacity

---

## 4.8 From Time Management to Attention Management

Traditional productivity tools focused on calendars and to-do lists.

AI-first productivity focuses on:

- Reducing context-switching

- Automating low-leverage tasks

- Surfacing insights *before* you ask

- Nudging people to focus on what matters most

**Example**: An AI agent notices a dip in web traffic, runs diagnostics, and recommends actions — before your marketing team even notices.

---

## 4.9 Measuring AI-Driven Productivity

Track impact with AI-specific KPIs:

| Dimension | Example Metric |
| --- | --- |
| Efficiency | Hours saved per team per month |
| Output | Volume of tasks/content delivered |
| Accuracy | Reduction in errors or corrections |
| Speed | Time to complete tasks or processes |
| Creativity | New ideas or variations produced |
| Strategic Value | % of time spent on high-leverage work |

Productivity is not just *doing more*. It's doing the *right* things, faster and better.

---

## 4.10 The Human-AI Partnership

Great productivity comes from synergy, not substitution:

- AI handles scale and repetition

- Humans focus on meaning, empathy, complexity

- The handoff between AI and humans becomes a core workflow design

Organizations must train teams in **collaborative intelligence** — knowing when to trust, override, or refine AI output.

---

## 4.11 Overcoming Barriers to Productivity Multiplication

Common roadblocks include:

- **Tool fatigue**: Too many AI tools, not enough integration

- **Poor change management**: Teams don't understand "why" AI is being used

- **Over-automation**: Losing the human touch

- **Mistrust of AI**: Fear of job loss, errors, or surveillance

Solutions:

- Pick fewer, more integrated tools

- Show productivity gains with data

- Keep humans in the loop

- Create feedback loops to improve AI tools over time

---

## 4.12 Scaling Productivity Without Scaling Burnout

AI-first orgs don't ask people to do more — they ask AI to do the *busy work*. Result:

- More time for strategy, reflection, and creativity

- More room for asynchronous deep work

- Higher satisfaction from focusing on meaningful impact

This isn't productivity theater — it's sustainable performance.

---

## 4.13 Real-World Examples of 10x Productivity

**Startup: 3-person marketing team using GPT, Notion AI, Canva AI**

- Went from 1 blog/week to 5

- Increased MQLs by 200%

- Cut content production cost by 80%

**Enterprise: Global insurance firm**

- AI triaged claims, flagging anomalies

- Reduced claims processing from 10 days to 2 hours

- Repurposed analysts for fraud detection

**SMB: Boutique law firm**

- GPT-based assistant drafted case summaries

- Admins used AI for scheduling and follow-ups

- Lawyers spent 40% more time with clients

---

## 4.14 The Future of AI-Enhanced Productivity

- **Multi-Agent Workflows**: Teams of AI agents collaborating across tools

- **Proactive Productivity**: AI anticipates your next task

- **Productivity as a Platform**: Unified AI layers across orgs

- **Custom Copilots**: Trained on your internal knowledge base

The real productivity unlock isn't *more AI* — it's *smarter integration* and *deeper alignment with people*.

---

## Conclusion: Working Smarter, Not Harder

The productivity multiplier offered by AI isn't optional. It's the only way to compete in a future where speed, intelligence, and personalization win.

AI-first organizations aren't asking people to do more. They're giving people **superpowers** — so they can do better.

In the next chapter, we'll explore how this productivity transforms not just teams, but entire ecosystems of communication and innovation.

# Chapter 5: Communication and Innovation in the AI Era

## Introduction: Why Communication and Innovation Go Hand in Hand

Communication is not just about talking. It's about alignment, clarity, and trust. Innovation is not just about ideas. It's about implementation, iteration, and cross-functional creativity.

In AI-first organizations, these two domains are converging. AI is revolutionizing how people **share knowledge, make decisions, brainstorm ideas, and bring new concepts to life.**

To unlock the full power of artificial intelligence, organizations must rethink how their people communicate — and how that fuels their capacity to innovate.

---

## 5.1 The Traditional Bottlenecks of Communication and Innovation

In legacy organizations, communication is often:

- **Slow** (email back-and-forths, delayed approvals)

- **Fragmented** (messages lost across Slack, email, docs)

- **Hierarchical** (decisions flow top-down)

- **Non-inclusive** (quiet voices and remote workers are sidelined)

Innovation, as a result, suffers:

- Brilliant ideas die in silos

- Feedback is delayed or absent

- Experiments are costly and slow

- Collaboration becomes a friction point

AI removes these bottlenecks — but only if we redesign for it.

---

## 5.2 The AI Communication Layer

AI introduces a new layer between humans and information:

- **Summarization**: Compress long reports into actionable insights

- **Translation**: Break down language barriers instantly

- **Sentiment Analysis**: Detect mood and tone in real time

- **Context Awareness**: Understand who needs what and when

- **Content Generation**: Draft emails, reports, proposals on the fly

This isn't about eliminating human communication. It's about making it **faster, sharper, and more focused.**

---

## 5.3 From Information Overload to Intelligence Amplification

The modern worker faces a deluge of information:

- 100+ Slack messages/day

- Dozens of emails

- Multiple dashboards and tools

AI filters the noise, surfaces the signal, and helps you act.

**Examples:**

- A sales manager gets a daily AI briefing summarizing lead activity.

- A project manager receives a synthesized update from five parallel conversations.

- A CEO gets a weekly sentiment score on employee morale based on internal comms.

The right information, at the right time, in the right tone — this is AI-first communication.

---

## 5.4 Reinventing the Meeting with AI

Meetings are ripe for disruption.

AI-first orgs now deploy:

- **Live Transcription** and **Summarization**

- **Automated Action Item Extraction**

- **AI Note-Takers** that tag topics and speakers

- **Knowledge Graphs** generated from discussion content

Results:

- Fewer, faster, more focused meetings

- Better follow-through

- Instant knowledge capture across teams

Meetings stop being time sinks and start becoming productivity multipliers.

---

## 5.5 Enabling Global Collaboration

AI tools break down barriers across:

- **Language** (real-time translation)

- **Time Zones** (asynchronous AI assistants)

- **Cultures** (tone and context adaptation)

- **Formats** (voice to text, text to chart, chart to insight)

A global product team can brainstorm, build, and ship with no lost motion — because AI becomes the glue that binds them.

---

## 5.6 Creating a Shared Organizational Brain

In AI-first companies:

- Conversations become **data**

- Meetings become **knowledge assets**

- Feedback loops become **self-improving systems**

AI tools map and connect this information to create a **dynamic organizational memory**:

- Searchable past decisions

- AI-recommended best practices

- Pattern recognition across projects

It's like giving your company a second brain — searchable, scalable, and smart.

---

## 5.7 From Linear to Networked Innovation

Traditional innovation is linear:

1. Idea

2. Pitch

3. Approval

4. Funding

5. Build

6. Launch

AI-first innovation is networked and recursive:

- Ideas emerge from AI-surfaced gaps or patterns

- Instant prototyping via no-code tools

- Continuous A/B testing and iteration

- Feedback from users → AI analysis → roadmap updates

Innovation is no longer a department. It's a *real-time, full-org function*.

---

## 5.8 AI in the Creative Process

Whether it's designing a product, writing an ad, or drafting a strategic plan — AI is a co-creator:

- Generate first drafts

- Brainstorm alternatives

- Remix concepts from different domains

- Suggest improvements based on prior successes

AI fuels **combinatorial creativity**: blending ideas from across industries, markets, and functions to produce something novel.

---

## 5.9 Multi-Agent Collaboration: The Future of Workflows

Teams of humans will soon work alongside teams of AI agents. Each agent might:

- Monitor customer sentiment

- Track competitor pricing

- Suggest feature updates

- Write code or design UI

- Coordinate with vendors

Human team leads become **orchestrators of intelligence** — directing flows of value rather than micromanaging tasks.

---

## 5.10 Innovation Accelerators: Prototyping with AI

What used to take weeks now takes days:

- Mockups from Midjourney or Uizard

- Landing pages from AI website builders

- User research from synthesized reviews and feedback

- Code from Copilot or GPT-based code agents

The cost of trying something new has dropped near zero. So **why not try more, faster**?

---

## 5.11 Building an Innovation Flywheel

The flywheel framework for AI-first innovation:

1. **Observe** – AI analyzes data, trends, behaviors

2. **Ideate** – AI suggests opportunities or problems to solve

3. **Prototype** – Teams build with AI tools

4. **Test** – Feedback captured, analyzed, looped

5. **Scale** – Successful ideas are scaled with AI systems

Each cycle strengthens the next. Innovation becomes a habit, not a project.

---

## 5.12 Redefining Roles: Communicators and Creators

In an AI-first world:

- Every employee is a communicator

- Every employee is a creator

- Every team is a lab

- Every product is a beta

**Cross-pollination** becomes standard:

- Finance collaborates with design

- Legal brainstorms with marketing

- AI suggests connections that humans miss

Collaboration is horizontal, not vertical.

---

## 5.13 AI-Augmented Decision-Making

The best decisions come from the blend of:

- Human intuition

- AI prediction

- Real-time feedback

AI-first orgs use:

- Scenario simulators

- Risk analysis engines

- Behavior modeling

- Consensus clustering

Boards, exec teams, and managers make smarter, faster, more accountable decisions.

---

## 5.14 Protecting Innovation from AI Risks

With great power comes great risk:

- **Groupthink via dominant AI models**

- **Bias in training data**

- **Overreliance on machine output**

- **Loss of human judgment**

Solutions:

- Diverse models and data sources

- AI ethics teams and review boards

- "Challenge AI" rituals in team meetings

- "Why did the AI say that?" as a standard question

Smart communication includes questioning the machine.

---

## 5.15 Case Studies: AI-Powered Communication and Innovation

**Netflix**

- AI suggests personalized thumbnails and trailers

- Content greenlighting powered by viewer behavior models

- Scripts analyzed for audience resonance

**Shopify**

- AI chatbot helps merchants solve issues 24/7

- Internal tools suggest pricing changes based on customer behavior

- Innovation pods use AI to ideate and validate product features

**IDEO**

- Uses generative AI in creative workshops

- Trains designers to "dance with the machine"

- Co-creation between humans and models normalized

---

## 5.16 Measuring Communication and Innovation Health

Track these metrics:

| Domain | AI-First Metric |
| --- | --- |
| Communication Clarity | % of AI-generated or summarized messages |
| Collaboration Speed | Time from idea to implementation |
| Innovation Volume | Number of tested ideas/month |

| | |
|---|---|
| Inclusion | Participation across levels/locations |
| Creative Output | Rate of new products, services, or campaigns |
| Sentiment | Morale and trust in tools, teams, and process |

AI adds visibility to communication dynamics and innovation pipelines.

---

## 5.17 Building Your AI-First Communication Stack

Suggested tools and approaches:

- **Chat + Collaboration**: Slack with GPT plug-ins

- **Meetings**: Otter.ai, Fireflies, Zoom AI Companion

- **Docs**: Notion AI, Google Docs AI

- **Design**: Canva AI, Figma AI, Midjourney

- **Coding**: GitHub Copilot, Code Interpreter

- **Research**: Perplexity AI, Scite, Consensus

- **Project Management**: ClickUp with AI workflows

Build an interoperable stack where humans and AI work side-by-side.

---

## Conclusion: Language Is Leverage. Creativity Is Currency.

Communication and innovation are not peripheral concerns. They are the *core capabilities* that define AI-first organizations.

With the right cultural practices and AI-enhanced systems, your teams can:

- Communicate faster and smarter

- Collaborate globally and inclusively

- Turn ideas into value at warp speed

The organizations that thrive in the coming decade won't just use AI. They'll speak its language — and create the future with it.

# Chapter 6: Unlocking New Growth Frontiers

## Introduction: Growth Is Being Redefined

Growth used to mean hiring more people, opening more offices, or spending more on advertising. It meant scaling linearly — more input for more output.

But in an AI-first world, growth is **no longer constrained by headcount, location, or time**. Today's most forward-thinking companies are discovering new frontiers of growth powered by artificial intelligence — frontiers that were unthinkable even a few years ago.

These aren't just efficiencies. These are **entirely new business models**, **markets**, **revenue streams**, and **value creation strategies.**

This chapter explores what it means to unlock growth through AI — not incrementally, but exponentially.

---

## 6.1 Traditional Growth vs. AI-First Growth

**Traditional Growth**

- Linear scaling of resources

- Market share battles in known categories

- Heavily reliant on capital expenditure

- Limited by human capacity

**AI-First Growth**

- Asynchronous, always-on capacity

- Rapid market expansion via digital channels

- Productized services and self-improving tools

- Scalable personalization and automation

- Exponential returns on data and intelligence

---

## 6.2 Growth as a Flywheel, Not a Funnel

AI-first companies don't just push customers through a funnel. They create **intelligent flywheels** — systems that learn, improve, and drive sustained momentum.

Example:

- Customer interacts → AI personalizes experience → Higher satisfaction → More data → Better insights → Better product/service → More engagement

This creates a **self-reinforcing cycle** of value creation.

---

## 6.3 Personalization at Scale = Conversion at Scale

One of AI's greatest growth levers is personalized engagement:

- Dynamic product recommendations

- AI-generated custom messaging

- Personalized pricing and offers

- Behavior-based content sequencing

**Case Study: Amazon**

- 35% of sales driven by recommendation engines

- Personalization drives retention, cross-sell, and loyalty

In an AI-first business, every user journey is **unique, dynamic, and optimized for growth.**

---

## 6.4 Turning Data into Revenue

Data used to be exhaust — a byproduct. Now it's **a product.**

AI-first organizations monetize data through:

- Predictive insights for internal use

- Selling anonymized data sets or market reports

- Licensing AI models trained on proprietary data

- Training custom agents for specific industries or clients

**Data x AI = New Business Lines.**

---

## 6.5 Productizing Knowledge

Knowledge workers once scaled linearly. Now, with AI:

- A top lawyer's analysis can become a 24/7 legal AI agent

- A therapist's guidance can be embedded in a mental health app

- A marketer's intuition can become a customer insights engine

This is **IP monetization at scale** — converting expertise into productized services.

---

## 6.6 AI-Driven Product Expansion

AI enables rapid testing, localization, and adaptation of products across markets:

- Translate content across languages in minutes

- Adapt offerings for regional trends and customs

- Run experiments across dozens of variables

Example: An education platform uses AI to instantly localize courses into 50 languages, unlocking new markets without new hires.

---

## 6.7 Unlocking the Long Tail of Customers

AI lets companies serve segments previously too small, too remote, or too costly:

- Microbusinesses

- Rural populations

- Niche enthusiasts

- First-time digital users

AI-first personalization means **the long tail is finally profitable**.

---

## 6.8 New Revenue Models Enabled by AI

AI enables entirely new monetization strategies:

### 1. Subscription Intelligence

- Smart pricing tiers based on usage and behavior

- Dynamic feature recommendations

- Automatic renewals and churn prevention

### 2. Usage-Based Models

- Pay-per-query, pay-per-insight, or API-based billing

### 3. Marketplace Models

- AI-powered platforms matching buyers and sellers (e.g. Upwork, Airbnb)

### 4. AI-as-a-Service

- Internal AI models licensed externally

---

## 6.9 Internal AI Agents = Infinite Scalability

Growth doesn't just come from revenue — it also comes from **reduced friction and cost.**

AI-first orgs scale with:

- AI sales agents generating and nurturing leads

- AI financial analysts forecasting and advising

- AI ops assistants managing logistics

Each agent is a **non-salaried, infinitely scalable team member.**

---

## 6.10 Innovation as a Growth Engine

AI supercharges innovation by:

- Accelerating R&D cycles

- Generating new product concepts

- Identifying unmet needs via behavior analysis

- Surfacing whitespace in the market

### Example: Pharmaceutical AI

AI cuts drug discovery timelines from 10 years to 2 — unlocking billions in revenue potential.

## 6.11 Hyper-Localization as a Growth Strategy

AI enables **ultra-targeted product variations**:

- Regional language AI chatbots

- City-specific marketing campaigns

- Culture-aware customer support

Global companies can **act local** — at scale.

## 6.12 Growth Through Ecosystem Building

AI-first companies often become **platforms**, not just products:

- APIs that others build on

- Developer ecosystems

- Community-driven data improvements

- App marketplaces powered by LLMs

Examples:

- Shopify's app ecosystem

- Salesforce Einstein's AI integrations

- OpenAI's plug-in architecture

Platform thinking = exponential network effects.

## 6.13 Turning Costs into Assets

AI transforms cost centers into growth assets:

| Traditional Cost | AI Growth Lever |
|---|---|
| Support team | AI chatbots and knowledge bases |
| HR department | AI recruiting, engagement analytics |
| IT helpdesk | Automated troubleshooting agents |
| Legal review | AI contract scanners |

These shifts free up capital for **R&D, expansion, and strategic bets**.

---

## 6.14 Growth Without Burnout

AI-first growth is sustainable because it reduces:

- Workload duplication

- Communication overhead

- Firefighting from poor data

Instead of grinding harder, teams:

- Focus on leverage

- Work with purpose

- Scale without stress

Growth doesn't have to mean burnout. It can mean **better work, more often.**

---

## 6.15 Case Studies: AI-First Growth in Action

### Case 1: A SaaS Startup

- Used GPT to automate support, onboard clients, write docs

- Grew user base 10x with zero new hires

### Case 2: A Manufacturing Firm

- AI forecasted demand, optimized inventory

- Freed up $3M in working capital, reinvested in R&D

### Case 3: A HealthTech Company

- AI triaged patients, routed to telehealth or in-person care

- Increased capacity 5x, with higher patient satisfaction

---

## 6.16 Challenges and Pitfalls to Avoid

- **Over-reliance on AI without human oversight**

- **Privacy violations in data monetization**

- **Scaling too fast without infrastructure**

- **Chasing vanity metrics over meaningful growth**

Sustainable growth requires **governance, ethics, and adaptability.**

---

## 6.17 Growth Metrics for AI-First Companies

Track both traditional and AI-specific indicators:

| Growth Dimension | Metrics |
| --- | --- |
| Revenue | MRR, LTV, CAC |
| Velocity | Time to market, iteration speed |
| Innovation | New products launched/quarter |
| Efficiency | Cost per transaction, AI agent ROI |
| Reach | Markets/languages served |
| Personalization | Conversion by segment or persona |

Don't just track more. Track smarter.

---

## Conclusion: Growth Without Limits

AI-first growth is not about doing what you've always done, slightly better. It's about **doing what was never possible before.**

It's about:

- Serving the underserved

- Productizing the invisible

- Turning ideas into industries

- Turning intelligence into income

This is the age of **exponential possibility**. And for those who embrace it, the question isn't how to grow — it's how far, how fast, and how meaningfully you can go.

# Chapter 7: The Democratization of AI

**Introduction: From Exclusive to Universal**

Artificial Intelligence was once the preserve of the elite — confined to research labs, billion-dollar companies, and tech geniuses. But something extraordinary has happened in the last few years: **AI has gone mainstream.**

We are now living through the **democratization of AI** — where powerful tools are:

- Accessible to everyone

- Affordable for small budgets

- Adaptable to local and niche needs

- Usable by people without technical backgrounds

This chapter will explore what it means when AI becomes a shared asset — and how individuals, startups, nonprofits, and small businesses can seize this historic opportunity.

---

## 7.1 What Is "Democratized AI"?

Democratized AI means:

- **Access**: Anyone with a smartphone or laptop can use AI tools

- **Affordability**: You don't need a million-dollar budget

- **Usability**: No PhD or engineering degree required

- **Customizability**: You can shape AI to your specific use case

- **Inclusivity**: Communities once excluded from innovation can now participate

In short: AI is no longer just for Google. It's for you.

---

## 7.2 How We Got Here: The Trends That Opened the Gates

Several tectonic shifts enabled AI's democratization:

### 1. Open-Source Ecosystem

- HuggingFace, TensorFlow, LangChain, and others have put powerful models in public hands.

### 2. Cloud Infrastructure

- AWS, Azure, and Google Cloud make scalable AI training affordable and accessible.

### 3. API Economy

- Plug-and-play AI models (like OpenAI's GPT or Stability's APIs) mean you don't need to build from scratch.

### 4. No-Code & Low-Code Platforms

- Tools like Zapier, Bubble, Peltarion, and Notion AI empower non-engineers to create with AI.

### 5. Language Models as Interfaces

- GPT and Claude allow anyone to "talk to" AI and get things done in plain English.

---

## 7.3 AI for Small and Medium Enterprises (SMEs)

Once locked out of advanced tech, SMEs now use AI to:

- Generate content and marketing copy

- Automate customer service

- Analyze customer data

- Optimize inventory

- Manage finances

**Case Study**: A bakery in Canada uses ChatGPT to write Instagram captions, respond to DMs, and brainstorm seasonal offers — all with a single person running the business.

---

## 7.4 AI for Startups: Leveling the Playing Field

Startups can now:

- Launch MVPs in days

- Build AI-driven apps with APIs

- Serve global audiences from day one

- Compete with large incumbents using smart agents

**Example**: A solo founder uses GPT, Midjourney, and Bubble to build and market a SaaS product, with zero full-time staff.

The AI-first startup is a new species of business: lean, fast, and global from birth.

---

## 7.5 AI for Nonprofits and Public Good

Democratization isn't just about profits — it's about **participation**.

AI is now helping nonprofits:

- Translate educational materials into local languages

- Analyze public health data

- Generate grant applications and donor reports

- Build bots that educate, advise, and mobilize

**Example**: A nonprofit in Kenya uses a WhatsApp chatbot to deliver agricultural advice to small farmers in Swahili, powered by open-source AI.

---

## 7.6 AI for Individuals: Empowering the Creator Economy

Every individual now has access to:

- Design tools (Canva AI, DALL·E, Midjourney)

- Writing assistants (Grammarly, Jasper, Notion AI)

- Business tools (ChatGPT, AI pitch deck creators, resume builders)

- Coding copilots (Replit, GitHub Copilot)

The result? **Solopreneurs, freelancers, and creators** are building businesses that once required teams of 10+.

---

## 7.7 Localization: Bringing AI to the Global South

AI democratization must be **global**. Key developments include:

- Language models trained in Hindi, Swahili, Bengali, Arabic, etc.

- Voice-first AI for communities with low literacy

- Offline AI for areas with limited internet

- Government and NGO partnerships for scale

**Initiatives**:

- Google's Project BARD in India

- Mozilla's Common Voice

- AI4D Africa programs

AI-first is no longer Silicon Valley's story. It's a **global movement.**

---

## 7.8 Education and Upskilling for All

Access means nothing without understanding. Democratized AI includes:

- Free courses (DeepLearning.AI, Google AI, Fast.ai)

- AI literacy toolkits for teachers and parents

- GPT tutors for students in underserved areas

- Community learning groups and AI hackathons

The future belongs to those who can **ask the right questions to AI** — not just write the code.

---

## 7.9 AI-First Infrastructure for the Masses

Companies and governments are now building:

- AI-powered digital public goods (e.g., identity systems, payment rails)

- Local language chatbots for essential services

- Data commons for inclusive model training

- Policies to promote open access and ethical AI

This is how we build **AI for the 99%, not just the 1%.**

---

## 7.10 The New AI Middle Class

Just as industrial revolutions created new working classes (mechanics, machinists, programmers), AI is creating:

- Prompt engineers

- AI workflow designers

- Model evaluators

- Data wranglers

- Solo AI entrepreneurs

These are the builders of the next economic era — and they can come from anywhere.

---

## 7.11 Challenges in Democratization

Despite progress, barriers remain:

- **Bias in models**: Most trained on English, Western datasets

- **Infrastructure inequality**: GPU access and internet speed disparities

- **Regulatory gaps**: Risk of exploitation, misinformation

- **Skill gaps**: Digital divides still exist

Solutions must be part of the movement:

- Local model training

- Equitable data collection

- Policy safeguards

- Ethical tool design

## 7.12 Governance for Inclusive AI

Democratization must include **democratic oversight**:

- Community participation in model shaping

- Transparency in datasets and algorithms

- Open audits and public input

- Empowering underrepresented voices in AI councils

We must **co-create AI** — not have it handed down from the top.

---

## 7.13 Case Studies: AI in the Hands of the Many

### Case 1: A Rural School in Nepal

- Teachers use GPT in Nepali to generate quizzes, translate lessons, and plan classes

- Students use voice-based AI tutors offline via local servers

### Case 2: A Creator in Nigeria

- Designs clothing lines using Midjourney

- Markets via AI-generated Instagram content

- Manages orders and customer chats with a WhatsApp bot

### Case 3: A Refugee-Led Startup

- Builds a chatbot in Arabic to help displaced people find resources

- Partners with local NGOs and uses open-source LLMs

---

## 7.14 Building an AI-Democratization Toolkit

What organizations can do:

- Curate free AI tools for different sectors

- Train local AI ambassadors

- Translate resources into local languages

- Partner with civil society

- Open-source your AI workflows and prompts

What individuals can do:

- Start a local AI learning circle

- Share how you use AI on social media

- Teach one person a week

- Challenge biased AI outputs

- Build tools for your community

---

## 7.15 Why Democratization Matters for Business

Even large companies benefit:

- Diverse input = better products

- Local innovators create unexpected breakthroughs

- Decentralized AI reduces costs and increases resilience

- Inclusive innovation is a **moral and strategic imperative**

If AI is for everyone, **innovation comes from everywhere**.

---

## Conclusion: AI for All, By All

The democratization of AI is not a technical trend. It's a civilizational shift.

When a student in Guatemala, a founder in Nairobi, and a nurse in Manila all use the same AI as a developer in San Francisco — we're building a world where intelligence is **not hoarded but shared**.

This is not about catching up to Silicon Valley. It's about building something better, together.

The future is not AI-powered by the few. It's **AI-powered by the many.**

# Chapter 8: Laying the Groundwork – Phase One

## Introduction: Start Small, Think Big, Move Fast

Becoming an AI-first organization isn't about launching with a bang or investing millions on day one. It's about **laying a smart, solid, and scalable foundation**.

Phase One is the most critical part of the transformation — it determines whether AI adoption becomes a core operating strategy or remains a failed experiment. Done well, it builds momentum, wins trust, and unlocks deeper layers of value. Done poorly, it sows confusion, fear, and resistance.

This chapter walks through the essential groundwork to prepare your organization — technologically, operationally, and culturally — to become AI-first.

---

## 8.1 The Three Pillars of AI-First Groundwork

1. **Assessment** – Where are you now?

2. **Alignment** – Where do you want to go?

3. **Activation** – What are the first real steps to take?

This isn't theory. It's a sequence designed for action.

---

## 8.2 AI Readiness Assessment

Before jumping into tools and integrations, ask:

**Cultural Readiness**

- Is there curiosity or fear about AI?

- Do employees trust leadership to guide transformation?

- Are teams encouraged to experiment?

**Technical Readiness**

- Do you have clean, structured, accessible data?

- What's your current stack (CRM, ERP, cloud)?

- Is your data siloed or interoperable?

**Leadership Readiness**

- Do executives understand the AI opportunity?

- Is there a C-level sponsor for AI initiatives?

- Is AI part of board-level conversations?

**Operational Readiness**

- Are workflows documented and measurable?

- Are you tracking KPIs that AI can optimize?

- Are there bottlenecks ripe for automation?

Use this assessment to build a **baseline AI scorecard**.

---

## 8.3 Set Clear, Strategic Objectives

AI initiatives fail when the goals are vague. Instead, define **business outcomes**:

- Reduce customer service costs by 30%

- Double marketing content output

- Increase employee engagement scores

- Improve onboarding efficiency by 50%

- Decrease financial forecasting time from weeks to hours

**Tie AI to business goals — not tech for tech's sake.**

---

## 8.4 Choose a Pilot Project with High Impact and Low Risk

Great first projects are:

- Visible but not mission-critical

- Repeatable and measurable

- Understood by leadership and staff

- Limited in scope, but scalable later

**Examples**:

- AI assistant for customer FAQs

- GPT-powered email summarizer for sales reps

- Auto-tagging system for support tickets

- Lead scoring model for outbound marketing

Start where success is **likely**, **tangible**, and **shareable**.

---

## 8.5 Build Your AI Core Team

Create a cross-functional AI task force including:

- A business champion (owner of the outcome)

- A data person (engineer or analyst)

- A project manager (to drive execution)

- A vendor or consultant (to speed up adoption)

- A few pilot users (for feedback and advocacy)

This is your **AI vanguard** — responsible for results, learning, and iteration.

## 8.6 Train for Fluency, Not Just Literacy

Training is not a one-time webinar. It's a mindset reboot.

**Tiered Learning Tracks:**

- **Executives**: Strategic value of AI, use cases, governance

- **Managers**: Workflow optimization, prompt engineering, change management

- **Employees**: How to use AI tools safely, ethically, and productively

Build confidence through:

- Live demos

- Internal AI office hours

- Use case storytelling

- Peer training and AI champions

## 8.7 Pick the Right First Tools

Don't start by building from scratch. Start with tools that:

- Integrate into existing workflows

- Require minimal training

- Are well-documented and supported

- Offer strong ROI

**Starter Tools**:

- ChatGPT Enterprise for ideation and content

- Fireflies or Otter for meeting notes

- Zapier + GPT for automating tasks

- Reclaim.ai for calendar optimization

- Claude or Perplexity for research

Don't chase novelty — chase **utility**.

---

## 8.8 Secure Buy-In Through Shared Wins

Early wins build credibility. Share them:

- "We saved 30 hours/month on email summaries."

- "We created 2x more content with 1/2 the effort."

- "We reduced response time by 50% with an AI helpdesk."

Use internal channels, team demos, and data dashboards. Let **results do the selling.**

---

## 8.9 Don't Over-Automate — Keep Humans in the Loop

AI-first does not mean AI-only. Guardrails matter:

- AI suggests, humans approve

- AI drafts, humans refine

- AI predicts, humans investigate

**Augmentation is the first phase.** Full autonomy comes later — and only where appropriate.

---

## 8.10 Track What Matters

Build a mini dashboard for your pilot:

| Metric | Description |
|---|---|
| Usage Rate | How often is the tool used? |
| Time Saved | Estimate in hours or minutes |
| Quality | Are outputs meeting expectations? |
| Satisfaction | Feedback from end users |
| Uplift | Measurable business improvement |

Share results early and often. Make progress **visible and tangible**.

---

## 8.11 Address Fear and Resistance

People fear AI for many reasons:

- "Will I lose my job?"

- "I don't understand it."

- "What if it makes a mistake?"

Your job is to:

- **Empathize**: Fear is normal

- **Educate**: Share stories of empowerment

- **Reassure**: Show augmentation, not replacement

- **Invite**: Make people part of the design and rollout

Culture eats strategy. And it also **eats fear**, if you feed it truth and trust.

---

## 8.12 Ethical Frameworks from the Start

Don't bolt on ethics later. Bake it in now:

- Review AI outputs for bias

- Document how decisions are made

- Be transparent with employees and customers

- Create opt-outs where appropriate

- Establish an internal AI ethics board or oversight group

Ethical use is not a box to tick. It's a **trust enabler** and competitive differentiator.

---

## 8.13 Plan for Feedback Loops and Iteration

The first pilot won't be perfect. That's the point.

Create:

- Feedback forms

- Regular retrospectives

- Open office hours

- "Kill the tool" policies if it fails

Celebrate failures that teach. Measure value over vanity.

---

## 8.14 Prepare for Scaling: What Comes Next?

As your pilot matures:

- Identify similar workflows in other teams

- Customize the same tools for different functions

- Evaluate platforms for enterprise-wide rollout

- Assign AI leads in each department

**Phase One is not the destination. It's the on-ramp.**

---

## 8.15 Build Your AI Playbook

Document:

- Tool setup

- Prompt templates

- Use case examples

- FAQs and lessons learned

- Escalation paths

Share it with new teams. Turn your success into a **scalable internal service.**

---

## 8.16 Case Studies in Groundwork Done Right

### Startup: Marketing Automation with GPT

- Used GPT to write social posts, emails, landing page copy

- Decreased cost per acquisition by 40%

- Playbook shared with other departments within a month

### Enterprise: Legal Document Summarization

- Used Claude to summarize contracts

- Lawyers reviewed for accuracy

- Cut review time by 70%

- Now deployed across 12 business units

### University: Research Assistant for Faculty

- GPT used to summarize papers, suggest citations

- Custom GPTs trained for each discipline

- Faculty engagement up 300%

---

## 8.17 Common Pitfalls in Phase One — and How to Avoid Them

| Mistake | Fix |
| --- | --- |

| | |
|---|---|
| Starting too big | Start with a single, clear workflow |
| Lack of champions | Appoint internal AI advocates |
| Skipping training | Run live demos, Q&As, office hours |
| Tool fatigue | Pick 1-2 tools only at first |
| No metrics | Build a dashboard before you launch |

Don't be perfect. Just be **intentional and iterative**.

---

## Conclusion: You're Not Behind — You're Just Beginning

AI-first doesn't require a massive leap. It starts with **one tool, one team, one workflow.**

Lay the groundwork with care, clarity, and courage. Every great transformation begins with a single, well-executed pilot. That's how movements — and revolutions — begin.

In the next chapter, we'll look at how to scale this momentum across departments and geographies — taking your AI-first mindset from pilot to platform.

# Chapter 9: Scaling AI Across the Organization

**Introduction: From Islands to Infrastructure**

You've launched your first AI pilots. You've seen the power of automation, augmentation, and acceleration. Now comes the next frontier — **scale**.

Scaling AI isn't about adding more tools. It's about building the systems, culture, governance, and infrastructure to make AI a **core operating layer** of your organization.

This chapter is a comprehensive roadmap for that journey — turning AI from a set of experiments into an enterprise-wide transformation engine.

---

## 9.1 From Pilot to Platform: What Scaling Really Means

Scaling AI means:

- Moving from isolated use cases to coordinated initiatives

- Making AI accessible to every function and role

- Creating standardized, secure, and governed platforms

- Embedding AI into daily workflows, not just innovation labs

- Unlocking **network effects** as AI tools connect and compound

It's not about doing more. It's about doing things **differently, consistently, and intelligently at scale.**

---

## 9.2 Why Most AI Pilots Fail to Scale

Common pitfalls:

- No executive mandate or budget to expand

- Tools don't integrate with core systems

- Lack of training and adoption across functions

- Misalignment between IT, ops, and business leaders

- Fear, fatigue, or resistance in the middle layers

Scaling AI is as much about **change management** as it is about tech.

---

## 9.3 The Three Layers of AI Scaling

### 1. Functional Scaling

AI in every department: HR, finance, sales, support, legal, marketing, product.

### 2. Technical Scaling

Centralized tools, data access, APIs, governance, security, infrastructure.

### 3. Cultural Scaling

Mindset shift across the workforce: curiosity, confidence, experimentation, ethical awareness.

You must scale **horizontally (departments)** and **vertically (depth of integration).**

---

## 9.4 Build a Central AI Enablement Team (AI Center of Excellence)

This cross-functional unit guides the scaling process. It includes:

- AI Strategy Lead (exec sponsor)

- Data Science/Engineering team

- Change management experts

- Cybersecurity and compliance reps

- Communications and training support

Responsibilities:

- Approve tools and models

- Provide education and support

- Share best practices and metrics

- Manage internal AI stack and resources

Think of it as **internal AI-as-a-Service.**

---

## 9.5 Create Department-Level AI Champions

Empower local "AI Sherpas" who:

- Identify use cases

- Guide adoption in their department

- Train peers and troubleshoot

- Give feedback to central AI team

These are not data scientists. They're trusted influencers who **bridge business and AI.**

---

## 9.6 Scale by Use Case Category, Not Just Tool

Rather than scaling specific apps, scale categories:

| Use Case Category | Examples |
| --- | --- |
| Communication | Meeting summaries, auto-email drafting |
| Productivity | Calendar optimization, workflow automation |
| Support | Chatbots, smart ticketing |
| Knowledge Management | Searchable internal wikis, AI research assistants |
| Insights | Predictive analytics, forecasting |
| Content | Blog generation, ad copy, reports |
| Talent | Resume screening, learning pathways |

This helps prevent tool sprawl and enables **modular, reusable workflows.**

---

## 9.7 Integrate AI Into Your Core Systems

To scale, AI must connect with:

- CRM (Salesforce, HubSpot)

- ERP (SAP, Oracle)

- HRIS (Workday, BambooHR)

- Project Management (Asana, Jira)

- BI/Analytics (Tableau, PowerBI)

- Collaboration (Slack, Teams, Notion)

Look for vendors with **native AI integrations** or **API openness**.

---

## 9.8 Train Everyone — Not Just "AI People"

AI at scale means:

- Non-tech employees using no-code AI tools

- Teams designing AI workflows

- Managers evaluating AI ROI

- Leaders understanding AI tradeoffs

Launch enterprise-wide learning programs with:

- E-learning modules

- Use case playbooks

- Certification paths

- Department-specific examples

Don't just train the few — **empower the many.**

---

## 9.9 Embed AI Into Standard Operating Procedures (SOPs)

If it's not in the SOP, it won't scale. Embed AI into:

- Onboarding checklists

- Marketing campaign processes

- Sales pipelines

- Support workflows

- Hiring procedures

Example: "Step 3: Use Claude to summarize candidate portfolio."

AI becomes part of the **muscle memory** of the organization.

---

## 9.10 Build AI Dashboards for Visibility and Alignment

Every leader needs to see:

- Where AI is being used

- How it's impacting KPIs

- What's being tested next

- What risks exist

Build real-time dashboards showing:

- Tool usage

- Productivity impact

- Sentiment and adoption

- Business ROI

Scaling requires **transparency and feedback loops.**

---

## 9.11 Manage AI Governance, Risk, and Compliance at Scale

As you scale, so do risks:

- Model bias

- Privacy violations

- Shadow AI tools

- Hallucinations and errors

Build guardrails:

- Approved tool lists

- Ethical use guidelines

- Model explainability standards

- Data governance and lineage tracking

- Regular audits and reporting

Scaling without governance is **building without blueprints.**

---

## 9.12 Avoiding Tool Sprawl: Consolidate Your AI Stack

Too many tools = confusion, redundancy, security risk.

Consolidate with:

- Core platform (e.g. Microsoft Copilot, Google Workspace AI)

- Secure model hosting (e.g. Azure OpenAI, Anthropic API, private LLMs)

- Enterprise prompt libraries

- Internal knowledge base agents

Think platform, not product.

---

## 9.13 Measuring the Impact of Scaling AI

Don't just track usage — track outcomes.

| Metric Type | Examples |
| --- | --- |
| Operational | Time saved, tasks automated, response time |
| Financial | Revenue uplift, cost reduction, margin gain |
| Strategic | Speed to market, innovation rate |
| Cultural | Adoption rate, engagement, sentiment |
| Risk | Model compliance score, audit logs, error rates |

AI should drive **visible, trackable business results.**

---

## 9.14 Create a Culture of Continuous Experimentation

At scale, you need a system for innovation:

- Dedicated time for testing new AI use cases

- Internal AI hackathons or labs

- Reward structures for experimentation

- Quick pilot → evaluate → promote or kill loop

Every team becomes a lab. Every quarter becomes an opportunity.

## 9.15 Internal AI Marketplace

As AI use cases grow:

- Catalog tools, prompts, workflows

- Let teams request or contribute solutions

- Create a searchable internal "AI App Store"

This prevents duplication and promotes **shared value creation.**

## 9.16 Change Management at Scale

Scaling AI changes how people:

- Work

- Make decisions

- Measure success

- Interact with systems and teams

Support this change with:

- Internal comms campaigns

- Leader toolkits

- Peer coaching

- Open feedback channels

People don't resist change. They resist **uncertainty and irrelevance.**

## 9.17 Case Studies in AI Scaling

**Enterprise: Global Consulting Firm**

- Started with proposal writing assistants

- Scaled to 23 AI tools in legal, finance, HR

- Now has internal AI academy and platform team

**University: Research Scaling**

- Faculty trained on GPT

- Summarization and literature review assistants launched

- Created custom GPTs per department

- Used centralized dashboard to monitor usage and ethics

**Retail: Omni-Channel Optimization**

- Scaled AI from marketing to ops

- AI now manages demand forecasting, pricing, and inventory

- Embedded in ERP and POS systems

- Doubled same-store profitability in 18 months

---

## 9.18 AI Scaling Playbook: A Step-by-Step Guide

**Step 1**: Form AI Center of Excellence
**Step 2**: Identify core categories to scale
**Step 3**: Train and assign AI champions
**Step 4**: Audit and consolidate AI tools
**Step 5**: Build AI-enhanced SOPs
**Step 6**: Launch dashboards and reporting
**Step 7**: Run experiments and promote wins
**Step 8**: Monitor risks, ethics, and security
**Step 9**: Maintain continuous improvement loop
**Step 10**: Celebrate AI-first transformation milestones

## Conclusion: Scaling Is the Shift from Excitement to Execution

Pilot projects are exciting. But scaling is where real transformation happens.

When AI moves from isolated tests to **an integrated operating system**, organizations:

- Work smarter

- Move faster

- Serve better

- Grow stronger

- Innovate endlessly

This is where your AI journey becomes permanent. This is where momentum becomes **strategy.**

In Chapter 10, we'll explore how to build the infrastructure — from data lakes to model ops — that powers your scaled, AI-first enterprise.

# Chapter 10: Building AI Infrastructure in Your Business

## Introduction: Infrastructure as the AI Growth Engine

AI is not just about intelligence — it's about **infrastructure**. Without the right foundation, even the smartest tools fail to deliver. Building AI infrastructure means designing systems that can ingest, process, analyze, act, and learn — continuously, securely, and at scale.

If you want AI to touch every function of your business, it must sit on a rock-solid backbone: from data architecture and model orchestration to governance, observability, and integration.

This chapter offers a step-by-step breakdown of how to build, scale, and manage the AI infrastructure that will support your business now and into the future.

---

## 10.1 What Is AI Infrastructure?

AI infrastructure is the **technical and operational foundation** that allows you to deploy, scale, and govern AI systems. It includes:

- **Data pipelines and storage** (e.g., lakes, warehouses)

- **Model training and serving environments**

- **APIs and integration layers**

- **Monitoring and observability**

- **Security and compliance systems**

- **Compute power and orchestration**

Think of it as the **AI equivalent of roads, bridges, and power lines** — invisible, but essential.

---

## 10.2 Why AI Infrastructure Matters

Without proper infrastructure, AI initiatives suffer from:

- Siloed or poor-quality data

- Inconsistent model performance

- Long deployment cycles

- Tool fragmentation

- High operational costs

- Security and compliance risks

Strong AI infrastructure makes innovation **repeatable, scalable, and safe**.

---

## 10.3 Core Components of an AI Infrastructure Stack

### 1. Data Infrastructure

- Cloud storage (AWS S3, Google Cloud Storage)

- Data lakes (Databricks, Snowflake, Delta Lake)

- ETL/ELT tools (Fivetran, Airbyte, dbt)

- Data cataloging and governance (Collibra, Alation)

### 2. Model Infrastructure

- ML platforms (SageMaker, Vertex AI, Azure ML)

- MLOps tools (Weights & Biases, MLflow, Metaflow)

- Model training orchestration (Kubeflow, Ray, Prefect)

- LLM-specific infrastructure (LangChain, Haystack, LlamaIndex)

## 3. Compute Infrastructure

- GPUs, TPUs, high-performance CPUs

- Auto-scaling clusters (Kubernetes, Slurm)

- Serverless AI (Lambda, Cloud Run)

## 4. Integration Layer

- APIs and SDKs for internal and external tools

- Event-based architectures (Kafka, Pub/Sub)

- Middleware for AI access control and throttling

## 5. Monitoring & Observability

- Model performance tracking

- Drift detection

- Data lineage visualization

- Alerting and incident response

## 6. Governance & Compliance

- Model versioning

- Explainability tools (SHAP, LIME, TruEra)

- Access controls, encryption, audits

- Documentation and traceability

---

## 10.4 Build vs. Buy: Strategic Decisions

Should you build custom infrastructure or buy off-the-shelf?

| Criteria | Build | Buy |
|---|---|---|
| Customization | High | Low |
| Speed | Slow | Fast |
| Cost | High upfront | Subscription |
| Maintenance | Internal team | Vendor-managed |
| Competitive Edge | Proprietary moat | Market parity |

**Recommendation**: Start with buying (PaaS), then build where you want **differentiation**.

---

## 10.5 Building a Scalable Data Foundation

Data is the fuel of AI. Your infrastructure should enable:

- **Real-time data ingestion**

- **Batch processing for historical analysis**

- **Data validation and cleansing**

- **Feature stores** for model input reuse

- **Metadata management** for discoverability

Best practices:

- Use columnar formats (Parquet, ORC)

- Adopt schema versioning

- Encrypt at rest and in transit

- Log all data transformations

---

## 10.6 Model Development Environments

Enable your data science team to:

- Access secure, scalable compute

- Run reproducible experiments

- Share model artifacts

- Automate retraining with fresh data

Set up:

- Git-based version control

- Containerized environments (Docker)

- Experiment tracking tools (MLflow, Neptune)

- CI/CD for ML (CI/ML pipelines)

Goal: **Move models from lab to production in weeks, not months.**

---

## 10.7 Serving Models in Production

Choose your architecture:

- Batch inference (e.g., nightly scoring jobs)

- Real-time inference (REST APIs)

- Streaming inference (real-time recommendations)

Optimize for:

- Latency (fast response)

- Throughput (many requests)

- Cost (GPU vs CPU vs serverless)

- Availability (auto-scaling, redundancy)

Model routers and gateways (e.g., BentoML, Seldon) simplify deployment.

---

## 10.8 Integrating with the Business Stack

AI must plug into your core systems:

- CRM (HubSpot, Salesforce): predictive scoring

- ERP (SAP, Oracle): demand forecasting

- HRIS (Workday, ADP): attrition prediction

- Marketing automation (Marketo, Mailchimp): content generation

- Customer support (Zendesk, Intercom): AI chatbots

Use APIs, webhooks, and prebuilt connectors to embed AI **where work happens.**

## 10.9 Managing Multiple Models and Agents

Most organizations need dozens of models:

- Forecasting

- Classification

- NLP

- Recommendation

- Personalization

- Anomaly detection

Set up:

- Model registry and metadata tracking

- Canary deployment strategies

- Multi-model A/B testing

- Agent orchestration tools (LangGraph, CrewAI)

Treat AI like **software infrastructure** — versioned, monitored, automated.

---

## 10.10 Security and Compliance in AI Infrastructure

AI introduces new risks:

- Model extraction

- Prompt injection

- Data leakage

- Adversarial inputs

Mitigate with:

- Role-based access control (RBAC)

- Prompt sanitization

- Anonymization and pseudonymization

- Security-focused LLM gateways (PromptLayer, Humanloop)

- Model "kill switch" capability

Comply with:

- GDPR, CCPA, HIPAA

- Sectoral audits and documentation

**Security-first AI infrastructure** is non-negotiable.

---

## 10.11 Observability and Feedback Loops

Track:

- Model accuracy and drift

- User satisfaction

- Prompt effectiveness

- Cost per inference

- Business KPIs linked to model output

Tools: Arize, WhyLabs, Fiddler, Truera

Use this data to:

- Tune prompts

- Retrain models

- Flag issues

- Drive product improvements

AI without observability is like flying blind.

---

## 10.12 People and Process Infrastructure

Technology needs humans to manage it.

Hire or upskill:

- MLOps engineers

- Prompt engineers

- Data product managers

- AI governance leads

- Business-AI liaisons

Define workflows:

- Model approval process

- Retraining triggers

- Incident response plans

**Infrastructure = tools + teams + trust.**

---

## 10.13 Total Cost of Ownership and Optimization

Track:

- Compute spend (GPU hours)

- Storage costs

- API usage (token billing)

- Engineering hours

Use:

- Spot instances

- Caching and vector databases (e.g. Pinecone, Weaviate)

- Model distillation or quantization

- Inference optimizers (ONNX, TensorRT)

Optimize for **value per dollar**, not just capability.

---

## 10.14 Multi-Tenant and Multi-Model Infrastructure

If you serve multiple business units or clients:

- Use namespace isolation

- Per-client vector indexes

- Role-based dashboards

- FinOps dashboards for billing and accountability

AI infrastructure must scale across **complex, federated environments.**

---

## 10.15 Case Studies in Scalable AI Infrastructure

**Case: Global Insurance Firm**

- Central data lake with fine-grained access control

- Deployed 87 models across 12 business units

- Created AI orchestration layer for triaging claims

- Saved $10M annually in processing costs

**Case: E-Commerce Brand**

- Real-time LLM pipeline for product recommendations

- AI-native CMS fed content to web, app, email

- Integrated observability tools for prompt quality

- Boosted average order value by 15%

---

## 10.16 AI Infrastructure Blueprint: 12-Component Checklist

1. Cloud Data Lake

2. Feature Store

3. Model Training Environment

4. Model Registry

5. Real-Time Inference Gateway

6. Agent Orchestration Layer

7. MLOps Pipelines

8. Prompt Management Platform

9. API Gateway + Integration Hub

10. Monitoring + Drift Detection

11. Security + Governance Framework

12. FinOps + Cost Control Layer

Build from **modular components**, not monolithic platforms.

---

## Conclusion: The Invisible Layer That Powers the AI Revolution

You don't see infrastructure. But you feel its impact everywhere.

AI infrastructure determines:

- How fast you can ship innovation

- How safe and ethical your AI is

- How resilient your systems are

- How much you can scale

- How far you can go

The future belongs to organizations that don't just use AI — but **build the infrastructure to let it thrive.**

In Chapter 11, we'll explore how to manage the risks and ethical challenges of AI — and build governance that scales with your ambition.

# Chapter 11: Risks, Ethics, and Future Trends

**Introduction: Progress Without Principles Is Peril**

Artificial Intelligence is the defining technology of the 21st century — but with great power comes great responsibility. As AI becomes embedded in the DNA of organizations, its impact on people, society, and the planet cannot be ignored.

Building an AI-first organization is not just about scaling innovation — it's about managing **risk**, **building trust**, and **defining your values** in a world that's moving faster than regulation can keep up.

This chapter explores the ethical frameworks, risk management strategies, and emerging trends that every leader must understand to deploy AI responsibly — and lead into the future with both confidence and conscience.

---

# Part I: Identifying the Risks

## 11.1 Data Risks

### 1. Bias in Data

- Historical data reflects societal bias (gender, race, income).

- Skewed datasets lead to skewed outputs.

- Example: AI rejecting job candidates based on biased training data.

## 2. Data Privacy and Consent

- GDPR, CCPA, HIPAA, and global data sovereignty laws.

- Risk of unauthorized use, re-identification, or data leakage.

## 3. Data Quality

- Dirty, inconsistent, or incomplete data leads to poor AI performance.

- "Garbage in, garbage out" still holds true in the age of GPT.

---

# 11.2 Model Risks

## 1. Hallucination and Fabrication

- LLMs can produce plausible but incorrect outputs.

- Especially dangerous in legal, medical, or financial use cases.

## 2. Lack of Explainability

- Black-box models are hard to audit or interpret.

- Users and regulators demand transparency.

## 3. Drift and Decay

- Models degrade over time as patterns change.

- Without monitoring and retraining, performance drops.

---

# 11.3 Operational and Business Risks

## 1. Over-Automation

- Automating processes that need human judgment (e.g., layoffs, loan approvals).

- Risk of alienation, poor decisions, or customer backlash.

## 2. Model Dependency

- Over-reliance on a single AI provider or model (vendor lock-in).

- Downtime or deprecation risk.

## 3. Misuse or Shadow AI

- Employees using unapproved tools.

- No visibility, no security, no accountability.

---

# 11.4 Security Risks

## 1. Prompt Injection Attacks

- Malicious users manipulate AI to leak sensitive info or bypass filters.

## 2. Adversarial Inputs

- Slight tweaks to inputs that cause incorrect classification or decisions.

## 3. Model Inversion and Extraction

- Attackers reverse-engineer models to steal training data or IP.

---

# 11.5 Societal and Reputational Risks

- Misuse of AI leading to discrimination or exclusion

- Public backlash over job displacement or surveillance

- Ethical violations becoming PR disasters

- "Deepfake" misuse, misinformation amplification

AI-first organizations must **go beyond legal compliance** to earn trust.

---

# Part II: Embedding AI Ethics into the Organization

## 11.6 Define an AI Ethics Framework

Start with 5 core principles:

1. **Transparency**: What AI is used, how it works, and why it made a decision.

2. **Fairness**: No discrimination based on race, gender, ability, or geography.

3. **Privacy**: User control, consent, and anonymization.

4. **Accountability**: Human-in-the-loop, auditability, and remediation mechanisms.

5. **Safety**: Proactive testing, monitoring, and red-teaming.

---

## 11.7 Create an AI Ethics Board or Committee

Responsibilities:

- Review AI use cases for alignment with core principles

- Approve high-impact deployments

- Serve as escalation point for concerns

- Ensure diversity of perspective (not just technical voices)

Include cross-functional reps from:

- Legal

- Product

- HR

- Marketing

- Engineering

- External advisors or community reps

---

## 11.8 Build Explainability and Transparency into Products

Tools and techniques:

- LIME, SHAP for feature attribution

- Model cards to document intended use, limitations, and metrics

- User-facing explanations: "Why did I see this recommendation?"

Transparency builds **trust, clarity, and accountability**.

---

## 11.9 Train and Empower Teams on Ethical AI

Include AI ethics in:

- Onboarding programs

- Manager training

- Product design reviews

- Engineering sprint planning

Use:

- Real-world case studies

- Scenario-based learning

- Internal certifications

- Regular refreshers and updates

Ethics must be **lived, not laminated**.

---

## 11.10 Red Teaming and AI Risk Simulation

Actively test your AI systems before attackers or failure modes emerge.

Scenarios:

- "What if our AI tool gave biased results in job screening?"

- "What if a customer uses our chatbot to harass others?"

- "What if our model suddenly degrades during a market shift?"

Use cross-functional teams to simulate risks — then build defenses.

---

## 11.11 Build Governance into the Infrastructure

AI ethics is not just about policies. It's about **code and control**.

Embed in:

- Model deployment pipelines

- Access control systems

- Logging and audit trails

- Monitoring dashboards

- Alerting systems

Compliance should be **continuous, automated, and adaptive**.

# Part III: Navigating the Future of AI Responsibly

## 11.12 The Regulatory Landscape Is Evolving

What's coming:

- EU AI Act (risk-tiered approach)

- US algorithmic accountability laws

- China's model registry mandates

- Industry-specific standards (FINRA, FDA)

Be proactive:

- Track laws early

- Participate in shaping them

- Align with global best practices

**Regulation is not the enemy — it's the floor of trust.**

## 11.13 The Rise of Responsible AI Certifications

Emerging frameworks and certifications:

- ISO/IEC 42001: AI Management Systems

- NIST AI Risk Management Framework

- Open Ethics Label Initiative

- Microsoft Responsible AI Standard

Benefits:

- Market credibility

- Enterprise sales qualification

- Talent attraction

- Compliance readiness

---

## 11.14 Open Source and Transparency Movements

AI is being democratized — and so is ethical development:

- Open source models (Meta's LLaMA, Mistral, HuggingFace)

- Public model evaluations (HELIA, TruthfulQA, BigBench)

- Citizen-led audits and red teaming

- Decentralized alignment efforts (e.g., EleutherAI)

Open ecosystems can **crowdsource safety and ethics**.

---

## 11.15 The Role of AI in Shaping Society

AI is not just a business tool — it's a social force.

- Reshaping education (AI tutors, personalized learning)

- Influencing public discourse (LLMs in journalism, misinformation)

- Changing governance (AI-assisted policymaking)

- Shifting geopolitics (AI in defense, surveillance, diplomacy)

Leaders must **step beyond the boardroom** to influence public policy and values.

## 11.16 Long-Term Risk: Misalignment and AGI

As models grow more powerful:

- How do we ensure alignment with human values?

- Who decides what "human values" are?

- What if models outpace human control?

Global initiatives are emerging:

- OpenAI's Superalignment

- Anthropic's Constitutional AI

- DeepMind's AI Safety research

**Responsible scaling is humanity's grand challenge.**

---

## 11.17 Ethical AI as Strategic Advantage

Ethical leadership creates:

- Brand trust

- Customer loyalty

- Employee engagement

- Regulatory resilience

- Partnership opportunities

- Long-term survivability

In a world of hype, ethics is your **anchor and amplifier.**

---

## 11.18 Case Studies in Ethical AI Leadership

### Salesforce

- Embedded ethical AI principles into all products

- Created AI Acceptable Use Policy

- Includes social scientists on ethics board

### Mozilla

- Built privacy-first AI for Firefox

- Funds open AI research in the public interest

- Promotes algorithmic transparency and control

### Unilever

- Uses AI for hiring — but added bias detection, explainability, and audit trails

- Trains HR staff on AI fairness

---

## 11.19 Questions Every Organization Should Ask

1. How are we identifying and mitigating bias?

2. Who is accountable when AI goes wrong?

3. Are we transparent about how AI affects users?

4. Have we included diverse voices in AI design?

5. Are we using AI in ways that align with our mission?

Build a **living ethics checklist** into every launch.

## Conclusion: A Future Built on Intelligence and Integrity

Being AI-first is no longer just a competitive advantage — it's a cultural, social, and moral responsibility.

The future is not AI vs humanity. The future is AI **for** humanity — but only if we build it that way.

As a leader, you must ask not only what AI can do, but also:

- What **should** it do?

- For **whom**?

- Under **whose values**?

- And **with what safeguards**?

That is the final frontier of becoming truly AI-first.

In Chapter 12, we'll chart a clear, actionable path forward — your personalized **roadmap to becoming an AI-first organization.**

# Chapter 12: Roadmap to an AI-First Business

**Introduction: From Ambition to Execution**

By now, you understand the transformative power of AI. You've explored the technology, the culture, the infrastructure, the risks, and the opportunities. But the real question remains:

**How do you get there — step by step?**

This chapter provides a complete, structured, and practical roadmap for becoming an AI-first organization. It's designed to guide CEOs, CTOs, heads of innovation, and transformation leaders through every phase — from initial experiments to enterprise-wide integration and strategic reinvention.

---

## 12.1 What Is an AI-First Organization? (Recap)

An AI-first business is one where:

- AI drives decisions at every level

- AI is embedded in workflows, not bolted on

- Data flows seamlessly and is actively used

- Humans and AI collaborate continuously

- Innovation is rapid, distributed, and evidence-based

- AI is not just a tool — it's a strategic core

This transformation is as foundational as electricity or the internet. It touches **technology, people, process, and philosophy.**

---

## 12.2 The Five Phases of AI Transformation

1. **Inspiration** – Understanding what's possible

2. **Initiation** – Starting pilots with structure

3. **Integration** – Embedding AI into workflows

4. **Institutionalization** – Building AI into the core

5. **Intelligent Reinvention** – Redesigning for the AI era

Each phase builds momentum, maturity, and strategic alignment.

---

## Phase 1: Inspiration – The Awakening

### 12.3 Leadership Exposure

- Host executive briefings on AI trends

- Analyze competitor AI strategies

- Invite futurists, AI researchers, and practitioners to speak

- Use demos to shift perception from hype to utility

**Outcome**: Senior leadership commits to exploring AI.

### 12.4 Company-Wide Awareness

- Town halls to introduce AI-first vision

- Myth-busting workshops (AI ≠ job loss)

- Highlight AI benefits for each department

- Create an internal microsite on AI strategy

**Outcome**: Early buy-in and cultural readiness.

---

# Phase 2: Initiation – Pilot and Learn

## 12.5 Launch Your First AI Projects

Select high-potential, low-risk use cases:

- Email summarization

- AI-based support ticket tagging

- Lead scoring in marketing

- Personalized onboarding in HR

Ensure projects are:

- Time-bound

- Measurable

- Sponsored by department leaders

- Supported by a small cross-functional team

**Outcome**: Proof points and confidence.

## 12.6 Build Your AI Core Team

Assemble your first AI unit:

- Business analyst

- Data engineer

- AI/ML specialist or vendor

- Process owner

- Project manager

Start small. Empower them to deliver **value fast.**

---

## 12.7 Measure, Share, and Repeat

- Track ROI: time saved, errors reduced, engagement lifted

- Document learnings and iterate

- Share results in internal newsletters, dashboards, or town halls

**Outcome**: Momentum spreads to adjacent teams.

---

# Phase 3: Integration – Embedding AI

## 12.8 Formalize Governance and Ethics

- Draft AI usage policies

- Create an AI ethics council

- Define red lines (e.g., no facial recognition, no surveillance use)

- Document where AI is used, why, and how

**Outcome**: Trust framework for responsible scale.

---

## 12.9 Expand AI Use Cases Across Departments

Sales:

- GPT-based proposal generators

- Predictive deal scoring

Finance:

- Auto-categorization of spend

- AI-generated forecasts

Customer Success:

- AI agents for 24/7 chat

- Sentiment analysis

HR:

- Resume screening

- Career pathway modeling

**Outcome**: AI becomes **normal** in daily operations.

---

## 12.10 Upskill and Educate

- Launch internal AI academies

- Offer role-based certifications

- Train managers to lead hybrid (human + AI) teams

- Incentivize AI innovation through rewards and recognition

**Outcome**: AI fluency across the organization.

# Phase 4: Institutionalization – Systematizing AI

## 12.11 Create a Center of AI Excellence

Functions:

- Tool vetting and procurement

- AI architecture and infrastructure design

- Security and compliance oversight

- Knowledge sharing

- Internal consulting

**Outcome**: AI becomes a **shared service** and internal platform.

---

## 12.12 Build or Consolidate Your AI Stack

Key tools:

- LLM platform (e.g., OpenAI, Claude, local LLMs)

- MLOps tools for model lifecycle

- Vector databases for semantic search

- Prompt libraries and template engines

- API gateway for cross-departmental access

**Outcome**: AI infrastructure standardizes and scales.

---

## 12.13 Launch Internal AI Marketplaces

- Prompt galleries by function

- Shared agents (e.g., "Meeting Summarizer," "Contract Review Bot")

- Templates and workflows

- User feedback and upvote features

**Outcome**: AI becomes **self-service.**

---

## 12.14 Monitor Impact Across KPIs

Build dashboards for:

- AI adoption rate

- AI ROI by use case

- Model performance metrics

- Employee satisfaction with AI

- Risk incidents and ethical issues

**Outcome**: Decisions become **data-driven.**

---

# Phase 5: Intelligent Reinvention – Rebuilding from the Core

## 12.15 Reinvent Business Models

Ask:

- What would our product/service look like if it were AI-native?

- Could we license our AI internally or externally?

- What new value chains could we create?

Examples:

- Turn data into insights-as-a-service

- Launch GPT agents as digital employees

- Use LLMs to create adaptive content, coaching, or diagnostics

**Outcome**: Growth and innovation shift from **linear to exponential**.

---

## 12.16 Rethink Organizational Design

Traditional: hierarchy + silos
AI-first: networks + AI agents + distributed decisions

Changes:

- Fewer layers of approval

- Cross-functional AI squads

- AI "teammates" in every department

**Outcome**: Work becomes faster, smarter, and more human-focused.

---

## 12.17 Transform Culture from Resistance to Reinvention

Key traits of an AI-native culture:

- Curiosity beats certainty

- Data beats intuition

- Transparency beats opacity

- Ethics beats shortcuts

- Learning beats perfection

**Outcome**: Cultural adaptability becomes your **superpower.**

---

# 12.18 Sample 12-Month AI Transformation Timeline

| Month | Milestone |
|---|---|
| 1 | Leadership alignment & AI vision |
| 2 | AI literacy bootcamps |
| 3 | Launch first 2 pilots |
| 4 | Begin AI ethics framework |
| 5 | Share early wins org-wide |
| 6 | Launch 5 new AI tools across 3 functions |
| 7 | Build internal AI playbook |
| 8 | Stand up AI center of excellence |
| 9 | Integrate AI into SOPs |
| 10 | Host AI innovation week |

| 11 | Start AI dashboarding |

| 12 | Present year-end review + roadmap 2.0 |

---

## 12.19 Common Pitfalls and How to Avoid Them

| Pitfall | Fix |
| --- | --- |
| Pilot purgatory | Set clear scale-up criteria |
| Tool overload | Standardize platform layer |
| Fear and resistance | Continuous education + empathy |
| Over-automation | Keep humans in the loop |
| Lack of metrics | Build dashboards from day one |

---

## 12.20 Leadership in an AI-First Era

To lead this journey, you must:

- **Think exponentially**

- **Communicate clearly**

- **Learn constantly**

- **Empower experimentation**

- **Champion ethics**

- **Redesign work for human-AI symbiosis**

Your mindset is the engine of your transformation.

---

## Conclusion: The Journey Is the Strategy

AI is not a project. It's not a department. It's not a trend.
It is the **new foundation of competitive advantage.**

Becoming AI-first is not about being perfect. It's about:

- Starting where you are

- Scaling what works

- Learning continuously

- Earning trust

- Leading with courage

The roadmap is yours to adapt. Your organization is yours to transform. The future is being built
— and **you are now ready to build it.**

# AI-First Organization Transformation Workbook

**Title:** Becoming an AI-First Organization
 **Format:** 12-Month Guided Workbook + Strategic Playbook **Purpose:** Help leaders, teams, and enterprises practically implement AI-first principles across technology, culture, process, and strategy.

## Table of Contents

10. AI-First SOP Templates

11. AI KPI Dashboard Guide

12. Executive Leadership Guide

13. Glossary of AI Terms

14. Resources & Further Reading

---

# 1. Overview & Executive Summary

This workbook distills the entire *Becoming an AI-First Organization* book into a pragmatic set of tools and templates. It's designed for:

- CEOs and Executive Teams

- Innovation & Digital Transformation Leaders

- Department Heads and Operational Managers

- HR, IT, and AI/ML Teams

**Key Principles:**

- Start small. Think exponential.

- Culture is infrastructure.

- AI is a co-worker, not a competitor.

- Ethics is the foundation.

---

# 2. AI Readiness Diagnostic (Self-Assessment)

Rate your organization on a scale of 1–5:

- Executive understanding of AI

- Departmental awareness and willingness

- Data quality and accessibility

- Workflow digitization

- Infrastructure readiness

- Budget allocation for AI initiatives

- Current AI tools in use

- Governance and compliance maturity

- Cross-functional collaboration

- AI training & literacy

**Score Guide:**

- 0–20: Foundational Phase

- 21–35: Ready to Pilot

- 36–45: Ready to Scale

- 46–50: AI-Embedded Enterprise

---

# 3. Phase-Based Transformation Framework

## Phase 1: Inspiration

- Executive briefings

- AI myth-busting town halls

- AI internal portal

## Phase 2: Initiation

- Launch 2–3 pilot projects

- Assemble cross-functional team

- Train initial champions

## Phase 3: Integration

- Embed AI into SOPs

- Department-wide rollout

- Launch AI dashboards

## Phase 4: Institutionalization

- Stand up Center of AI Excellence

- Consolidate AI stack

- Build internal AI marketplace

## Phase 5: Intelligent Reinvention

- AI-native business models

- Autonomous teams and agents

- Strategic reinvention workshops

---

# 4. 12-Month Transformation Timeline

**Month**                    **Milestone**

1      Leadership Alignment & AI Vision Workshop

2      AI Literacy Bootcamps

3      Launch 3 AI Pilots (Ops, CX, HR)

4      Begin Drafting AI Governance Framework

5      Early Wins Showcase

6      Deploy Tools Across 4 Departments

7      Build Internal Prompt Library

8      Launch AI Center of Excellence

9      Embed AI into SOPs Organization-Wide

10     Company-Wide AI Innovation Challenge

11     Launch Org-Wide AI Metrics Dashboard

12     Year-End Review + Next-Stage Strategy

# 5. Departmental AI Opportunity Maps

Includes templates and examples for:

- Sales

- Marketing

- Customer Support

- Human Resources

- Finance

- Legal

- Operations

- IT & Cybersecurity

Each map includes:

- Top 5 AI use cases

- Tools to consider

- KPIs to track

---

# 6. Ethics & Governance Checklist

- AI Acceptable Use Policy

- Transparent documentation

- Bias & fairness testing

- Human-in-the-loop safeguards

- Explainability protocols

- Regulatory compliance (GDPR, CCPA, etc.)

- Red team simulation exercises

---

# 7. AI Infrastructure Blueprint

- Data pipeline architecture

- Model deployment stack

- MLOps tools

- LLM agent frameworks

- Vector database recommendations

- Integration standards

---

# 8. AI Tools & Vendors Directory

Curated list of tools by category:

- Chatbots

- LLMs

- No-code AI

- Prompt orchestration

- Scheduling/assistants

- Research automation

- Customer success

- Forecasting engines

---

# 9. Use Case Templates

For each use case:

- Problem statement

- Proposed AI solution

- Target KPI

- Tool or model used

- Human-AI interaction plan

- Success criteria

---

# 10. AI-First SOP Templates

Standard operating procedures for:

- AI agent handoff

- Prompt testing & validation

- Workflow automation

- Escalation protocol

- Feedback loop design

---

# 11. AI KPI Dashboard Guide

Track metrics across:

- Productivity (time saved, output increased)

- Accuracy (error reduction)

- Adoption (tool usage by department)

- Engagement (employee sentiment)

- Strategic lift (revenue or cost impact)

---

# 12. Executive Leadership Guide

- CEO/CTO/CIO AI Playbook

- Talking points for board and investors

- Budgeting for AI at scale

- Measuring strategic return

- Handling resistance and fear

---

# 13. Glossary of AI Terms

Simplified definitions of:

- Machine learning

- Natural language processing

- Prompt engineering

- Fine-tuning

- Transformers

- MLOps

- AI governance

---

# 14. Resources & Further Reading

- Recommended books

- AI newsletters and media

- AI ethics organizations

- Online courses and certifications

- Open-source projects and communities

---

**Final Note:** This workbook is a living tool. Use it. Customize it. Share it. Iterate as your organization evolves.

AI isn't the future — it's the foundation of your competitive edge today.